John McCain

SERVING HIS COUNTRY

BARBARA SILBERDICK
FEINBERG

A Gateway Biography

The Millbrook Press
Brookfield, Connecticut

In memory of my beloved aunt
Ethel Steinberg Scheldon

Cover photograph courtesy of © Les Stone/Corbis Sygma

Photographs courtesy of Archive Photos: p. 4 (CNP/Ron Sachs); © Corbis Sygma: pp. 7, 11, 13, 14, 17, 19 (top), 32; U. S. Naval Historical Center: p. 9; AP/Wide World Photos: pp. 19 (bottom), 20, 25, 29 (left), 37; © Reuters NewMedia Inc./Corbis: pp. 22, 44 (both); © AFP/Corbis: pp. 23, 40; Corbis/Bettmann-UPI: p. 29 (right); Senator McCain: p. 34; *The Arizona Republic*: p. 35

Cataloging-in-Publication Data is on file at the Library of Congress
ISBN 0-7613-1974-3 (lib. bdg.)

Published by The Millbrook Press, Inc.
2 Old New Milford Road
Brookfield, Connecticut 06804
www.millbrookpress.com

CONTENTS

1
On the Move 4

2
In the Navy 12

3
In POW Camps 20

4
To the U.S. Senate 30

5
Along the Campaign Trail 40

Important Dates 45
Notes 46
Index 47

John S. McCain III

1

On the Move

John Sidney McCain III was born on August 20, 1936, at the Coco Solo Naval Air Base hospital in Panama. Members of his family had served in the American military ever since the War of Independence. One McCain was on General George Washington's staff. Others fought in the War of 1812 and in the Civil War, siding with the South. During World War I, a McCain organized the draft, requiring men to join the armed forces.

John's grandfather and father were the first of the family to go to sea. When John was born, his grandfather, John S. McCain Sr., was in command of the Coco Solo air base. His father, John S. McCain Jr., a submariner, was stationed nearby. Both became naval heroes during World War II and later retired as admirals.

John was not an easy child to raise. At about age two, he developed terrible temper tantrums and held his breath until he passed out. His anxious parents consulted a navy doctor. He advised them to place their son fully clothed in a tub of cold water. This harsh treatment worked. For the rest of his life, however, John would have problems controlling his temper.

At an early age, John learned what it meant to serve his country. Growing up in a navy family meant that his father and grandfather had less time to spend with him than he would have liked. Also it required him to be uprooted and to move around the country. He did not complain.

As children, John III, his older sister Susan, and his younger brother Joseph, saw very little of their father. John said, "I am certain that he wanted to share with me the warm affection that he and his father had shared. But he wanted me to know also that a man's life should be big enough [for] both duty to family and duty to country. . . . It was a hard lesson for me."[1] Even when his father was not at sea, he spent long hours on duty. On Christmas morning, for example, he left for work after the family opened their gifts.

The McCain family circa 1944: Roberta, Joe, John, Vice Admiral John S. (McCain's grandfather), Susan, and John S. Jr. (McCain's father)

How proud John was when his grandfather and father came to talk to his grade-school class in Vallejo, California. Because they were spending so much time at sea during World War II, he rarely got to see them. The visit showed how much they cared about him.

Like most navy wives, John's mother, Roberta Wright McCain, took over raising the children and running the household. She was the daughter of a wealthy Oklahoma oilman. She and her identical twin sister, Rowena, were beautiful and popular young women. She met John's father while she was a student at UCLA. They married in 1933 before she graduated.

"It is no surprise then that the personalities of children who have grown up in the Navy often resemble those of their mothers more than their fathers," John wrote.[2] From her, John got his love of talking, his cheerfulness, his spirit of adventure, his determination, and his streak of rebellion. He took on his sense of duty and honor from his father and his grandfather.

Like most navy families, the McCains moved whenever John's father was transferred to another base. Along the way, John's mother made sure that her children saw the natural and historic wonders of America. John wrote, "I recall being greatly impressed with Carlsbad Caverns, the Grand Canyon, . . . Washington's Mount Vernon, and Andrew Jackson's Hermitage."[3]

With each move, John attended a different school. He had to meet new teachers and make new friends. Sometimes, these teachers taught him things he had already learned elsewhere. At other times, they thought he knew things he had not yet studied. As the new kid in each school, John wanted to prove himself. Usually the shortest in his class, he picked fights with other boys.

His grandfather died suddenly, five days after the end of World War II, in September 1945. John had just turned nine. From then on, he treasured a photograph of his grandfather and father taken that September, the last time they were together. The next summer, John stayed with his widowed grandmother in Coronado, California. There he found his father's childhood books, includ-

Vice Admiral John S. McCain with his son Commander John S. McCain Jr. aboard a U.S. Navy ship at the time of the Japanese surrender in September 1945. Note the Japanese submarine in the background.

ing tales of King Arthur's Court and stories by Robert Louis Stevenson and Mark Twain. He claimed that "these works instilled in me a lifelong love of reading."[4] They encouraged him to seek out adventures of his own. They also taught him lessons about right and wrong.

In the fall of 1951, fifteen-year-old John was sent to Episcopal High School, an all-boys' boarding school in Alexandria, Virginia. Most of his classmates came from important southern families. He made little effort to follow the school's dress code and rules of gentlemanly conduct. He wore filthy blue jeans, a seedy jacket, and a ratty tie. He made himself into a little tough guy to show off his independence. His classmates responded by nicknaming him "McNasty." For him, this was a badge of honor. In defiance of school rules, he repeatedly snuck off at night with a few pals to visit the less respectable parts of Washington, D.C., and met girls. John had no desire to fit in.

However, he became a good wrestler and joined the junior varsity football team. The football coach was William Bee Ravenal III, a teacher. "He saw something in me that others did not. And he took a personal interest in me and we spent a good deal of time together."[5] John applied himself in Ravenal's English class and did well. He also enjoyed his history classes.

John aced the entrance exam for the U.S. Naval Academy at Annapolis. His classmates were surprised by his decision to attend Annapolis. He had never discussed his plans for the future

McCain (front row, third from right) in a high school photograph from his senior year

with them or with his parents. However, he knew that his family had always expected him to go the Naval Academy. Early in the summer of 1954, his father drove him to Maryland to begin his naval training.

2

On the Navy

The Naval Academy prepared McCain for service to his country. He performed well during his first summer at Annapolis, then an all-male school. He became an undefeated boxer, marched in formation, and eagerly took part in training exercises. He even temporarily became a company commander.

With the start of classes in the fall, he began to disappoint his superiors at the academy. He was bored by math and engineering classes and did not pay attention. Only government, history, and English courses interested him. However, McCain had to take daily quizzes, and exams every other week. He successfully crammed the material his friends taught him. According to one of them, "he only wanted to know enough to get by."[1]

Always independent, John McCain did not submit easily to hazing. Upperclassmen, called midshipmen, bossed and humiliated first-year students, known as "plebes." In those

McCain in a Naval Academy portrait

days, the academy encouraged hazing to find out who could endure harsh treatment. This trained plebes to be able to command under pressure. Like his classmates, John was required to memorize "Reef Points," a handbook of naval trivia. Midshipmen expected him to stand at attention and quote the handbook accurately whenever they questioned him. He had to run errands for them day or night, treat them with respect, and keep his uniform spotless. McCain found it hard to submit to midshipmen's demands. He was often punished.

McCain and his father at the Naval Academy at Annapolis

He also received demerits, low marks for conduct. Company commanders graded students on leadership skills, including personal appearance. McCain earned many demerits for being tardy and sloppy. Once Captain McCain unexpectedly dropped by his son's messy room. John and his friends were in the middle of a water balloon fight. His father lectured him in private: "You're in too much trouble here, Johnny, to be asking for any more."[2] This was the only time his father bawled him out for his poor record.

More often than most plebes, McCain endured solitary marches and other penalties. He later commented, "I wondered if I was being picked out of a crowd because of my last name."[3] (Some thought he got into Annapolis because of his family background, not on his own merit.) More likely, McCain was disciplined because he refused to fit in.

As a midshipman, he became the ringleader of the "Bad Bunch." They challenged Annapolis's rules. They slipped out at night to go drinking or to meet women. They had a few close calls. Yet they were never caught. His former roommate said that his friends "pretty much cared about his approval and they cared about what he thought."[4]

On the other hand, McCain proved his worth on sea duty. In the summer of 1957, during a training cruise to Rio de Janeiro, Brazil, the captain trained him to steer the ship. To the amazement of the other officers and his classmates, he did well.

In 1958, McCain graduated fifth from the bottom of his class. His class ranking was lowered because of his many demerits for misconduct. His father and his grandfather had also had poor records at the academy. Yet, both proved to be brave and heroic leaders. McCain intended to follow in their footsteps.

He decided to become a navy pilot, like his grandfather. He reported to Pensacola Naval Air Base in Florida and learned to fly. John spent more time partying than studying flight manuals. Nevertheless, he qualified to be sent for advanced training to Corpus Christi, Texas. One Saturday morning, his engine failed, and his plane hit the water. Knocked unconscious, he came to just as the plane settled on the bottom. He managed to open the canopy and swim to the surface. He had no serious injuries and soon got back to work—and play.

From 1960 to 1964, he was a carrier pilot, serving on the USS *Intrepid* and the USS *Enterprise*. He volunteered for extra duties and qualified to steer the aircraft carriers at sea. Yet he was a daredevil, too. Once he flew too low, cutting some power lines in Spain. The story of blacked-out cities made embarrassing newspaper headlines at home.

In 1964, he was reassigned to Pensacola on the staff of the Chief of Air Base Training. Most young officers would have welcomed this desk job. McCain, however, was eager for combat. "Nearly all the men in my family had made their reputations at war. It was my family's pride."[5] A successful combat record could

McCain (front row, second from left) aboard the USS *Intrepid* with members of his fighting squadron lead to command of a ship or an air squadron. The Vietnam War (1964–75) was just starting. American armed forces were trying to prevent the Communist North Vietnamese from taking over the Republic of South Vietnam.

Having been at sea, he had to wait his turn for active duty again. So he became a flight instructor to get more flying time. He was assigned to McCain Air Base in Meridian, Mississippi, named for his grandfather. Once, when he had been waved off from a landing, the impatient McCain radioed the control tower, "Let me land, or I'll take my field and go home."[6] His humor was not appreciated.

While at Pensacola, he met the Philadelphia model Carol Shepp. She was divorced from one of his Annapolis classmates. They soon developed a serious relationship. He flew from Meridian to Philadelphia most weekends to see her. On July 3, 1965, McCain married her in a quiet ceremony at the home of her friends. He adopted her sons, five-year-old Doug and three-year-old Andy in 1966. On September 2, 1966, Carol gave birth to a daughter, Sydney.

That December, on a return flight to Meridian, the engine on McCain's plane flamed out. He ejected himself from the plane and was not injured. The accident made him more impatient for combat duty—before something else happened. In the spring of 1967, Lieutenant Commander McCain was assigned to the aircraft carrier USS *Forrestal*, bound for Vietnam.

Flight instructor John McCain (front right)

McCain, his mother Roberta, and his father Rear Admiral John S. McCain Jr. at the dedication of the Admiral John S. McCain U.S. Navy training base

The fire on the USS *Forrestal* killed 134 crewmen.
McCain was able to escape.

3

On POW Camps

On July 29, 1967, a terrible explosion rocked the flight deck of the *Forrestal*, 60 miles off the coast of Vietnam. Fires broke out, destroying the planes and blowing up the rockets they carried. An electrical spark in a loose wire on deck had caused the disaster. It set off one of the rockets on Lieutenant Commander McCain's plane, an A-4E Skyhawk, a small bomber. He was already strapped into the cockpit, about to fly a combat mission over Vietnam.

McCain being rescued from a Hanoi lake after his plane was shot down by a North Vietnamese missile. Both his arms and his right knee were broken when he ejected from the failing plane.

Surrounded by burning fuel, McCain climbed out onto the nose of his plane, leaped into the flames, and rolled to safety. His thighs and chest were studded with bits of flying metal. Yet he was lucky. The accident took 134 lives and injured hundreds more.

McCain was posted to the USS *Oriskany*. His new squadron bombed installations around Hanoi, the capital city of North Vietnam. He wanted to prove himself in combat. On October 26, 1967, McCain eagerly set out on his twenty-fourth mission. His A-4E was struck by a SAM missile and lost its right wing. He radioed, "I'm hit," and ejected from the bomber.[1]

He landed in a lake in the center of the city. His right knee was smashed, and both his arms were broken. Vietnamese soldiers dragged him to shore. There an angry crowd of civilians kicked

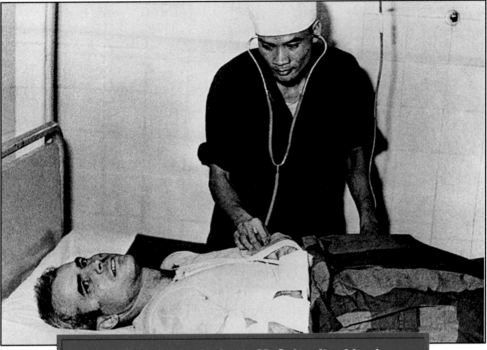

This 1967 photograph shows McCain after his plane crash in Hanoi. The North Vietnamese said he was treated well after his capture. McCain said he was beaten by a mob and bayoneted in the groin.

and spit at him. One soldier jabbed his ankle and groin with a bayonet. Another slammed a rifle butt into his shoulder. With the arrival of photographers, a woman offered him a cup of tea. Their pictures were meant to show that he was being well treated.

The captured navy pilot was taken to the Hoa Lo prisoner of war (POW) camp. POWs had nicknamed it the "Hanoi Hilton," contrasting its horrible conditions with the American luxury hotel chain. The Vietnamese promised to give McCain medical treatment in exchange for military information. He refused. Following the Military Code of Conduct, he stated his name, rank, and serial number. He was repeatedly questioned and beaten. Badly wounded, he was left to die.

Some days later, a prison official ordered his removal to a hospital. The Vietnamese had learned that he was the son of an admiral. The hospital was unsanitary and ill-equipped. McCain was never bathed or shaved. His room was infested with roaches. Doctors slapped a cast on his chest. They were unable to set his arms, but they did operate on his knee.

A few weeks later, he was moved to a cleaner room. The commander of the prison camps brought in a French television correspondent to interview McCain. Despite prompting by the commander, he refused to apologize for the bombing raids. Nor would he thank the Vietnamese for his "humane" medical treatment. At least, he recorded a brief message for his family. Then he was taken to his old room to face more questioning and beatings. He was getting weaker.

His captors moved him to a prison, nicknamed the "Plantation." It had been the garden of the official home of Hanoi's mayor. There his caring cellmates saved his life. They fed him and bathed him. One of them claimed, "I've seen some dead that looked at least as good as John."[2] It wasn't until early 1968 that he could walk on his own.

Years after McCain was held captive in Hoa Lo prison—the Hanoi Hilton—he was part of a visiting U.S. delegation to recognize the 25th anniversary of the end of the war in April 2000. It was his eighth trip back to Vietnam. Jack McCain is behind his father.

The prisoners were forced to listen to American antiwar speeches piped over the camp loudspeakers. By this time, well-known Americans like the actress Jane Fonda and the pediatrician Benjamin Spock were speaking out against the war. They did not think the United States should interfere in another country's civil war. American students rioted and protested, shouting, "Hell no, we won't go." They and millions of others looked for ways to avoid required military service. Some illegally left the country.

That spring, McCain was placed in solitary confinement, away from all other prisoners. He would not let this defeat him. He learned a complicated code of knocks on the walls to communicate with other prisoners. They shared information. Like the other POWs, he carefully memorized the names of the other 600 or so captives. No one trusted the Vietnamese to report all the men they held. To keep his sanity and his identity, McCain deliberately insulted the guards. In return they beat him—but not too hard. He soon found out why.

In June 1968, the commander of the camps offered to let him go home. The Code of Conduct required that prisoners held the longest be released first. So he refused to leave. Unknown to him, his father had just been made commander in chief of all the American forces in the Pacific. The Vietnamese had wanted to release McCain to embarrass the admiral.

As a result of McCain's decision, he was punched, pinned to a chair with ropes tied tightly around his broken arms, and left alone through the night. He was given no food and only a little water. After four days of this torture, he agreed to give his captors the confession they wanted. He wrote: "I am a black criminal and I have performed deeds of an air pirate."[3] It was taped and played over the camp loudspeakers. McCain wrote, "I was ashamed. I felt faithless, and couldn't control my despair."[4] Yet many other prisoners had broken under torture, too. McCain was dragged back to his cell.

From 1969 on, the POWs were permitted to write home once a month. In their letters, the men developed code words to pass the names of other POWs to their families. One letter writer asked his wife to say "hi to cousin King, Mc, Abel and his brother."[5] This was a reference to McCain. The prison guards, however, rarely gave letters or packages from home to the men.

McCain spent a total of 31 months in solitary confinement. Finally, in December 1970 his captors placed him in a large room with more than 50 other Americans. The POWs called it "Camp Unity." To keep up their spirits, the men gave each other classes in literature, math, and social studies. For relaxation, McCain told them the plots of hundreds of movies, some he had never seen.

A year later, he and some other ringleaders held a church service. For this offense, they spent more than six months in a punishment camp. It was known as "Skid Row," for its filthy conditions, tiny cells, and awful food. Then they were taken back to Camp Unity.

The POWs looked forward to war's end. In 1972, they cheered when bombs fell on Hanoi. In January 1973, the Paris peace talks brought about a cease-fire. In February, the POWs were shipped out, the earliest captured leaving first. Before their release, they were given new clothes and better food. Being a POW made McCain love his country even more. By surviving and refusing to embarrass his father, he had served his country.

On March 14, 1973, McCain arrived at Clark Air Force Base in the Philippines for medical treatment and debriefing, discussing his experiences. He learned that his wife had been in a serious auto accident in 1969. She had required 23 operations over the next two years to regain the use of her legs. They talked over the phone. After five and a half years, they were finally reunited at his homecoming in Jacksonville.

McCain wanted to remain on active duty. He underwent three months of hospitalization in Florida to fix his knee, his shoulder, and his arms. (He would never again be able to raise his arms above his chest to comb his hair.) During a tour of duty at the Naval War College, near Washington, D.C., he underwent painful physical therapy twice a week.

From 1974 to 1977, he served as an executive officer and then as commander of the Replacement Air Group (RAG) 174 in Jacksonville, Florida. He was in charge of training carrier pilots and crews at the navy's largest squadron. It had a history of fatal accidents. Under McCain's leadership, his first command, RAG won its first award for excellence. His next assignment was at the U.S. Senate, in a post his father had once held.

Lieutenant Commander John S. McCain III, March 18, 1973, with his wife Carol and son Doug in Jacksonville, Florida. McCain was finally released after being held prisoner over five years.

McCain shaking hands with President Richard Nixon, May 24, 1973, at a reception for former prisoners of war at the State Department. When he retired from the Navy, McCain had been awarded the Silver Star, the Bronze Star, the Legion of Merit, the Purple Heart, and the Distinguished Flying Cross.

4
To the U. S. Senate

From 1977 to 1981, Captain John McCain served as naval liaison to the U.S. Senate. Usually liaison officers were just errand boys, arranging overseas trips for politicians and traveling with them. McCain was different. Former Senator Gary Hart explained, "He was current on the issues . . . and he was very funny."[1] Senators often dropped by his tiny office in the Capitol to relax.

He also had a serious side. In 1978, backed by senior officers, McCain quietly helped senators block President Jimmy Carter's plans to replace large aircraft carriers with smaller ones. They all thought this would weaken American power overseas.

In the late 1970s, McCain went through a difficult time at work and at home. His injuries prevented him from serving in further active duty. In 1976, he had briefly thought about retiring and going into politics. After watching the Senate at work, he gave it more serious thought.

At the same time, his marriage was falling apart. In 1980, he and Carol were divorced. On May 17, he married Cindy Hensley, the daughter of a wealthy Arizona beer distributor. She was eighteen years younger than he was. Shortly after his father's death, on March 22, 1981, McCain finally resigned from the navy. Yet he still wanted to serve his country.

Settling in Phoenix, Arizona, he went to work for his father-in-law, doing public relations. He traveled around the state and gave many speeches for the beer company. This helped him meet important people and learn more about Arizona. He was preparing to run for political office.

In March 1982, eleven months later, he entered the Republican primary election in Arizona's First Congressional District. He hoped to be chosen as the party's candidate. His opponents accused him of being an outsider, lacking roots in the state. He explained that the navy moved him from state to state for most of his life. Then he said, "As a matter of fact, when I

John McCain and Cindy Hensley on their wedding day, May 17, 1980

think about it now, the place I lived longest in my life was Hanoi."[2] Ringing doorbells in 110-degree heat, McCain attracted supporters. He easily won the primary race. He swept the general election that followed.

In Congress, he was a loyal conservative Republican. He opposed government spending, gun control, abortion, and laws to protect the environment. He voted for measures to strengthen U.S. defense, to cut taxes, and to aid big business. He wanted the states, rather than the federal government, to make more decisions affecting citizens' lives.

Yet in September 1983, he voted against his party. He could not support President Ronald Reagan's plan to send U.S. Marines to war-torn Lebanon. Reminded of Vietnam, McCain did not think Americans should become involved there, and said so. One month later, a terrorist bomb blew up the marine barracks in Beirut, the capital city of Lebanon, killing more than two hundred servicemen. Over the years, McCain's independent opinions on military and other matters continued to displease both Republican and Democrat leaders.

Keeping a campaign promise, he spent every weekend in Arizona, giving speeches, meeting with voters, and marching in parades. It is no wonder that he was reelected to the House of Representatives in 1984. In December that year, Cindy gave birth to their daughter Meghan. In 1986, their son Jack was born. Another son, Jimmy, was born in 1988, and in 1992, the McCains

Congressman John McCain with wife Cindy and Meghan and Jack

adopted one-year-old Bridget from an orphanage in Bangladesh. In 1988, Cindy had founded the American Voluntary Medical Team (AVMT) to treat poor sick children all over the world. She found Bridget during a visit to Bangladesh with AVMT.

McCain won election to the U.S. Senate in 1986. His temper, however, did not help him win friends among the other ninety-nine members. Following Senate customs, he was expected to treat opponents with respect. Yet he blew up at Alabama Senator Richard Shelby for opposing President George Bush's nominee for secretary of defense, John Tower. There were other angry outbursts. Since then, he claimed to have gained more self-control. "Now I don't do that."[3]

In 1989, he had to defend himself in a political scandal, which involved the "Keating Five." Five senators, including McCain and former astronaut John Glenn, were accused of asking federal banking officials to be lenient with Charles Keating. His Lincoln Savings and Loan Association was being investigated. The bank soon failed, wiping out the savings of many elderly Americans.

Things looked bad for McCain. He said, "My honor was being questioned."[4] Keating had contributed money to his election campaigns. The McCains had been Keating's guests in the Bahamas and had often flown on his corporate jet. The records proving that they had paid for all those flights disappeared. Meanwhile, as a result of back surgery, Cindy McCain became addicted to painkillers. She recovered a few years later.

The Senate Ethics Committee decided to hold public hearings. McCain produced checks to show that he had paid for other trips on Keating's plane. He told the Ethics Committee that he met once with the federal bank officials, only to make sure that a citizen of his state was being treated fairly; and that he had not told the officials to go easy on Keating. They supported his statements.

Finally, in February 1991, McCain (and Glenn) were cleared of misconduct. McCain was scolded for using poor judgment in meeting with the bank examiners. He admitted, "I should never have even gone to those meetings. It gave the appearance of impropriety [wrongdoing]."[5]

Left to right: Senators John Glenn, Dennis DeConccini, and John McCain arrive at the Senate Ethics Committee hearing room to begin proceedings investigating the Keating Five.

Despite the scandal, McCain was reelected to the Senate in 1992, and again in 1998. As a senator, he voted the same way he had as a conservative congressman. By 1999, the Senate approved at least 234 laws he had proposed, according to his campaign Web site. Until 1996, McCain had loyally voted with his party 93 percent of the time.[6] Yet he broke with his party on two important issues: campaign finance reform, changing the way politicians and parties get money for elections; and the tobacco settlement, making the tobacco industry pay for the harm done to smokers.

In 1994, he and Democrat Wisconsin Senator Russ Feingold took up campaign finance reform. They wanted to ban "soft money," unlimited funds given to political parties. (The amounts of money given directly to candidates are limited by law.) Soft-money contributors included businesses, unions, and other special interests, like the National Rifle Association and the National Education Association, which wanted special treatment from the government. The two senators also tried to outlaw political ads paid for by special interests. These were often biased and misleading. Congress repeatedly failed to pass the McCain-Feingold Act.

McCain also wanted to discourage teenagers from smoking. In 1998, he fought to raise the taxes on cigarettes as part of the government's settlement with the tobacco industry. The industry had misled the public for years about the dangers of smoking. As chairman of the powerful Commerce Committee, McCain had pushed his scheme through the law-making process. Then the tobacco companies spent millions of dollars on political issue ads, attacking his plan. The Senate voted against McCain's tax plan. His reforms had angered many Republican senators. Both parties depended on soft money and political ads from special interest groups at election time.

The senator was proudest of another reform, his effort to reduce "pork barrel" projects. Senators selfishly spent taxpayers' money to benefit their own states. They added these projects to important laws, without having them debated in the full Senate. McCain's Web site, www.itsyourcountry.com, listed many examples of "pork," including "$750,000 for grasshopper research in Alaska."[7] In 1996, McCain had pushed through Congress a line-item veto act to end pork barrel projects. It let presidents remove unnecessary spending from measures about to become laws. In 1998, however, the Supreme Court overturned the act.

In 1999, McCain opposed President Bill Clinton's planned air war over Serbia. The Serbians had been murdering Albanians in Kosovo to gain control of the area. After the war began, reporters and television talk-show hosts asked McCain for his opinions. Drawing on his own experience, the senator urged that planes be allowed to fly low. That would prevent the bombing of innocent civilians. He also wanted ground troops to be sent in.

As a result of the president's policies, no American lives were lost in the air raids. However, on March 31, the Serbs captured three American soldiers in nearby Macedonia. This happened just a few days before McCain announced that he was running for president. On April 6, the senator made a statement to the press: "While now is not the time for the celebratory tour I had planned, I am a candidate for president, and I will formally kick off my campaign at a more appropriate time." Since his days as a POW, he had dreamed of becoming president to serve his country.

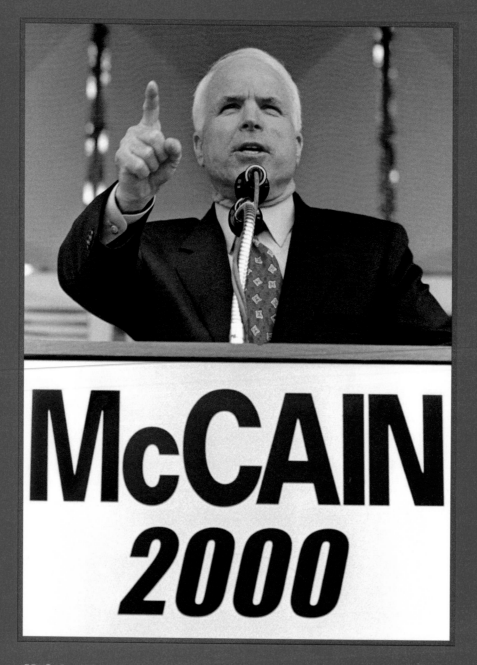

McCain announcing that he will run for the presidency of the United States in 2000

5

Along the Campaign Trail

During summer 1999, McCain traveled around the country on a book tour. He had just written *Faith of My Fathers*, describing how his grandfather's and father's naval careers influenced his life. His story was so powerful that people crowded into bookstores to meet him. They began to praise his moral character, his honesty, and his bravery. What a way to launch a campaign for president!

McCain appealed to the public as a reformer. He wanted to give government back to the people. He spoke out forcefully against the influence of special interests on lawmakers and public officials. The senator urged Americans to demand that Congress now pass the McCain-Feingold Act. He wanted to get rid of pork barrel laws too.

McCain campaigned as a "man of the people." He visited hundreds of town meetings and local gatherings. One woman said, "You ask him a question, and he answers it directly. He is obviously very well informed. He's a very effective speaker—he's got a lot of energy."[1] People felt that they could approach him, and that he would listen to what they had to say. They felt that he cared. He also took part in televised debates.

His message of reform attracted independent voters and Democrats to his cause. In many states, they could take part in Republican primary elections. However, members of the Republican party failed to support McCain. Despite his conservative voting record in the Senate, they felt he was not conservative enough. They heard him offer to protect Social Security, the government payments to retired people. They heard him promise to pay down the national debt, money the government owed, instead of making large tax cuts. To them, he sounded like a Democrat.

McCain lashed out at leaders of right-wing Christian groups, all loyal Republicans. These leaders had attacked McCain's co-campaign chairman, calling him a "vicious bigot"—a nasty intolerant person.[2] They urged their members not to vote for McCain.

During the primaries, Republicans supported his main opponent, Texas Governor George W. Bush. Bush, a son of President George Bush, had long been the choice of most party officials. They had developed a network of people ready to get out the vote. This put McCain at a disadvantage.

McCain had his own advantages. Unlike other candidates, he made himself constantly available to reporters and correspondents. He invited them on board his campaign bus, called the "Straight Talk Express." His conversations with them were humorous and blunt. He was open about himself and shared his misadventures as well as his successes with them. They responded by giving him widespread coverage. This saved him expensive publicity and helped make him a popular candidate. Instead of depending on large donations from wealthy Republicans and special interests, McCain was able to raise much of the money he needed by appeals on his Web site.

On "Super Tuesday," March 7, 2000, eleven states held primary elections. These elections chose delegates to the national Republican Convention. (The convention meets every four years to choose the party's nominees for president and vice president.) Democrat and Independent voters gave McCain victories in New Hampshire, Michigan, Connecticut, Rhode Island, Vermont, and Massachusetts. He had won earlier races in New Hampshire and Michigan. However, the total number of delegates prepared to nominate him fell far short of the 1,034 he needed. On March 9,

McCain withdrew from the contest for the Republican presidential nomination.

McCain went back to the Senate. He promised the public to fight for reform. "We will never give up this mission. I give you my word on that." This American hero would continue to serve his country.

McCain speaking to reporters after his "Super Tuesday" loss (above)

McCain gets back to work as senator

IMPORTANT DATES

1936	John S. McCain III born in the Panama Canal Zone.
1954–1958	Attends U.S. Naval Academy and graduates as ensign.
1958–1960	Receives training to become naval pilot.
1960–1964	Serves as carrier pilot on board the USS *Intrepid* and the USS *Enterprise*.
1965	Marries Carol Shepp.
1966	Adopts Carol's two sons, Douglas and Andrew; daughter Sydney born.
1967	Survives explosion aboard USS *Forrestal*; shot down over Hanoi and begins 5 1/2 years as prisoner of war.
1973	Released from POW camp.
1973–1974	Posted to Naval War College.
1974–1977	Serves as executive officer, then commander of Replacement Air Group 174 in Jacksonville, Florida.
1977–1981	U.S. Navy Liaison Officer to U.S. Senate.
1980	Divorces Carol; marries Cindy Hensley.
1981	Retires from U.S. Navy.
1982	Elected to House of Representatives.
1984	Daughter Meghan born; reelected to House of Representatives.
1986	Son Jack born; elected to U.S. Senate.
1988	Son Jimmy born.
1991	Cleared by the Senate Ethics Committee for past dealings with Charles Keating.
1992	Reelected to the U.S. Senate; adopts daughter Bridget from Bangladesh orphanage.
1997	Becomes chairman of the U.S. Senate Committee on Commerce and Transportation.
1998	Reelected to U.S. Senate.
1999	Announces intention to run for president of the United States.
2000	Withdraws from race for the Republican presidential nomination.

NOTES

Chapter 1

1. Michael Duffy and Nancy Gibbs, "Fathers, Sons, and Ghosts," *Time* (February 28, 1999), p. 41.
2. John McCain and Mark Salter, *Faith of My Fathers* (New York: Random House, 1999), p. 51.
3. McCain, *Faith of My Fathers*, p. 101.
4. McCain, *Faith of My Fathers*, p. 107.
5. Robert Timberg, *John McCain: An American Odyssey* (New York: Touchstone, 1999), p. 31.

Chapter 2

1. Robert Timberg, *The Nightingale's Song* (New York: Touchstone, 1996), p. 42.
2. McCain, *Faith of My Fathers*, p. 151.
3. Duffy and Gibbs, *Time*, p. 41.
4. Timberg, *The Nightingale's Song*, p. 34.
5. McCain, *Faith of My Fathers*, p. 162.
6. McCain, *Faith of My Fathers*, p. 21.

Chapter 3

1. McCain, *Faith of My Fathers*, p. 189.
2. Timberg, *John McCain: An American Odyssey*, p. 84.
3. Timberg, *The Nightingale's Song*, p. 136.

4. McCain, *Faith of My Fathers*, p. 244.
5. McCain, *Faith of My Fathers*, p. 281.

Chapter 4

1. Nicholas D. Kristof, "POW to Power Broker, A Chapter Most Telling," *New York Times* (February 27, 2000), p. A 32.
2. Timberg, *The Nightingale's Song*, pp. 303–304.
3. John F. Dickerson, "In This Corner . . . ," *Time* (November 15, 1999), p. 40.
4. Joe Klein, "Flawed Hero," *The New Yorker* (January 17, 2000), p. 32.
5. Ibid., pp. 32–33.
6. David Gramm, "The Hero Myth," *The New Republic* (May 24, 1999), p. 9.
7. Adam Clymer, "For McCain, Concerns in the Senate Are Subtle," *New York Times* (March 4, 2000), p. A11.

Chapter 5

1. Klein, "Flawed Hero," p. 29.
2. David Barstow, "McCain Denounces Political Tactics of the Christian Right," *New York Times* (February 29, 2000), p. A 16.

INDEX

Page numbers in *italics* refer to illustrations.

American Voluntary Medical Team (AVMT), 35

Bangladesh, 35
Bush, George, 35, 43
Bush, George W., 43

Campaign finance reform, 37–38
Carter, Jimmy, 31
Civil War, 5
Clinton, Bill, 39
Coco Solo Naval Air Base, Panama, 5, 6

DeConccini, Dennis, 37

Episcopal High School, Alexandria, Virginia, 10

Faith of My Fathers (McCain), 41
Feingold, Russ, 38
Fonda, Jane, 26

Glenn, John, 36, *37*

Hart, Gary, 30
Hazing, 13
Hoa Lo prisoner of war (POW) camp, 23–24, *25*, 26–27

Keating, Charles, 36
Keating Five scandal, 36–37

Kosovo, 39

Lebanon, 33

Lincoln Savings and Loan Association, 36

Macedonia, 39
McCain, Andrew, 18
McCain, Bridget, 35
McCain, Carol Shepp, 18, 28, *29*, 31
McCain, Cindy Hensley, 31, *32*, 33, *34*, 35, 36
McCain, Douglas, 18, *29*
McCain, Jack, 25, 33, *34*
McCain, Jimmy, 33
McCain, John S., Jr., 6–8, *7*, *9*, 11, *14*, 15, 16, *19*, 31, 41
McCain, John S., Sr., 6–9, *7*, *9*, 16, 41
McCain, John Sidney, III, *4*
   birth of, 5
   campaign finance reform and, 37–38
   childhood of, 6–10
   as congressman, 31, 33
   decorations, 29
   education of, 10, 12–13
   Faith of My Fathers by, 41
   as flight instructor, 18, *19*
   high school photograph of, *11*
   Keating Five scandal and, 36–37
   marriages of, 18, 31, *32*

at Naval Academy, 10–13, *14*, 15–16
Naval Academy portrait of, *13*
as naval liaison to U.S. Senate, 28,
   30–31
as navy pilot, 16, *17*, 21–22
nickname of, 10
pork barrel projects and, 38–39, 42
as presidential candidate, 39, *40*,
   41–44
as prisoner of war, 22–24, 26–28
resignation from Navy, 31
revisits Hanoi, 25
as senator, 35, 37–39, 44
temper of, 6, 35
tobacco industry and, 38
torture of, 26–27
McCain, Joseph, 6, 7
McCain, Meghan, 33, *34*
McCain, Roberta Wright, 7, 8, *19*
McCain, Susan, 6, 7
McCain, Sydney, 18
McCain Air Base, Meridian,
   Mississippi, 18
McCain-Feingold Act, 38, 42
Military Code of Conduct, 24, 26

National debt, 42
National Education Association, 38
National Rifle Association, 38
Nixon, Richard, *29*

Pensacola Naval Air Base, Florida, 16

Pork barrel projects, 38–39, 42

Ravenal, William Bee, III, 10
Reagan, Ronald, 33
Replacement Air Group (RAG) 174, 28
Republican National Convention
   (2000), 43–44

Senate Commerce Committee, 38
Senate Ethics Committee, 36, *37*
Serbia, 39
Shelby, Richard, 35
Social Security, 42
Spock, Benjamin, 26
Stevenson, Robert Louis, 10

Tobacco industry, 38
Tower, John, 35
Twain, Mark, 10

U.S. Naval Academy, Annapolis, 10–13,
   14, 15–16
USS *Enterprise*, 16
USS *Forrestal*, 18, *20*, 21
USS *Intrepid*, 16, *17*
USS *Oriskany*, 22

Vietnam War, 18, 21–24, 26–28

War of 1812, 5
Washington, George, 5
World War I, 5
World War II, 6, 7
Wright, Rowena,